Healing One's Addiction

How to Take Back Control of Your Life - Survival Guide for Codependents

Kelly Craig

Copyright © 2020 by KellyCraigBrands.com

Find out how to begin to love yourself and heal through spiritual practices and gain strength in living with your loved one's addiction:

www.kellycraigbrands.com

Join our community on Facebook where others are finding self-love in codependency.

http://bit.ly/2Raj9RN

Learn the tools you need to take back control of your life and to heal through Kelly's teachings. One-on-One Coaching and Group Coaching is available now at http://kellycraigbrands.com/services/

TO MY READERS....

I know how much it hurts. I know the pain and the guilt you are living with. You deserve better than what your loved one is offering you right now. We don't always understand the whys of addiction, which makes coping with it even more difficult.

I will be offering you my truth, my heart, and most importantly tools and strength to heal your life. The courage to move past your loved one's addiction and to let go and detach with love.

TABLE OF CONTENTS

To my readers....	2
Introduction	5
Chapter 1. When is Enough Enough, and How Do We Begin to Change it?	24
Chapter 2. Breaking the Cycle of Codependency	47
Chapter 3. Healing Through Fear	66
Chapter 4. Forgiveness and Serenity	85
Chapter 5. Trust in a Higher Power	95
Chapter 6. Get a Support System!	116
About The Author	121
Other Books By Kelly Craig	123
One Last Thing...	125

INTRODUCTION

I'd like you to know a bit about me so you can understand why I wanted to write this book for you.

There is hope beyond what you think. I believe your thoughts are just thoughts and they can be changed. I believe that each of us is connected to a higher power. You have greatness inside of you. I believe you were born with a destiny and that you can achieve your destiny and soar to new infinite possibilities despite any and all obstacles.

I was born December 12, 1972, premature and underweight. Back then you weren't allowed to leave the hospital until you were 5 lbs. It took a couple weeks, but I went home to my family on December 26th, and so the journey began.

Most babies don't have memories of their time spent in their cribs, at least, I hope not. However, I have vivid memories. I was left in there all day, painting the walls with poop, and rocking my crib over to the door, calling out, in hopes that someone would come to get me. My sisters, who are 10 and 13 years older than I am, tell the story of how they would do their best to care for me. Each day, I would be there waiting for them to come home from school so they could rescue me from my crib. They would get me dressed and make sure I had something to eat. They both suffer so much hurt to this day, feeling like they didn't do enough for me, but, at 10 and 13, what would one expect?

You may ask, "Where were her parents?" My dad had his own business as a pharmacist; he worked long hours and was not home much. I can't recall any memories of him from my very early childhood. As for my Mom, she was in bed, an alcoholic who didn't get up to take care of me.

At two years old, my Dad got remarried to my stepmother, Ann. In the divorce my sisters went to live with my Dad, and my brother and I stayed with my Mother.

Because my Mom was not able to afford our family home without income from my Dad we ended up moving to our other home on Cape Cod. We were not there for very long for financial reasons. My Mom and I ended up moving to my Gram's house and my brother went to live with my Dad.

My Gram's house was a two-family home and my Aunt lived upstairs with her family. They pretty much took on the role of helping to raise me until I was in second grade.

I remember being six years old and failing the eye tests at school. I had to have two eye operations, glasses, and a patch. I hated having to rotate my patch from eye to eye each day. I remember crying every morning thinking that everyone would make fun of me at school. This was my first real experience, that I remember, of not feeling good enough.

My Mom decided to move out of my Gram's when I was halfway through second grade. Her choice was a trailer park in the city to be closer to her job. So, my brother and I were uprooted once again as he was shifted back to my Mom because he was always in trouble. I was always with my brother and his friends because my Mom was either at work or too drunk to care for me. Throughout my younger years, my brother, who is seven years my elder, and I were really close. I did everything he did and went everywhere he went, for the most part, even hanging out in his room with him and all his friends while they drank beer and smoked pot, among other things. I pretty much saw it all as a kid.

My Mom was dating a couple of men and, right before I was to start third grade, she announced we were moving again with her new boyfriend back to our family home where it had all started for me. Only I didn't even know we had this home. I couldn't recall living there as a baby and only remembered living with my Gram before we moved to the trailer. It turned out that my Mom had been renting it all those years to another family. It was a nice big home with a back yard and a swimming pool in a nice town. My parents built it before I was born, and I had lived there until I was two.

So we packed, and I started at yet another school, a couple days into third grade. It was a great neighborhood, so all the kids just played in the streets or hung out at each other's houses. It was way better than living in a trailer park in the city.

But in reality, my experiences in this home consisted mostly of big alcohol-soaked parties, sleepless nights, and an absent mother. Living there was a very independent experience. I would wake up alone, prepare for school alone, and venture out to the bus alone. After school, I would step off of the bus, venture into my mom's room, lay on the bed and become immersed in *Sesame Street* and *Mister Rogers* until someone came home.

One night, the phone rang and I answered. it was my Dad. He asked where my Mom was and I informed him she wasn't home. He sternly instructed me to listen, "Kelly, I'm sending a police officer to the house. I want you to let him in when he gets there and wait with him until I come to get you, okay?" I murmured a coherent "yes" and hung up. As the officer arrived, so too did my mother and her boyfriend, Jim. When I told them what was going on, they were so angry. The officer arrived and came in to check on me. I was crying and confused. I convinced him I was okay, and he left. I was peering out my mom's window waiting for my dad, when eventually he pulled into the driveway in his white Porsche. Next, I saw my Mom's boyfriend walk up to the front of the car, lift it up off the ground and then drop it on the ground with my Dad still in it. I watched in horror as my dad backed out of the driveway. I didn't even get to say hi to him. Tears were streaming down my face. I couldn't understand why this was happening. Why was being alone such a big deal today? All I could think was that I got him in trouble and let him down. I was eight years old.

I remember my brother's 16th birthday at this house. My Mom bought him a keg of beer and there was a huge party. Needless to say, his 16th birthday party didn't end for three days. There were constant flows of teenagers and young adults around my house at all times. Our house was "the party house." But all fun things must come to an end, I guess.

By the time I was in fifth grade, my Mom announced we were moving again. This time to Las Vegas. My oldest sister, who was around 21 at the time, had left home to move there and had a baby so my Mom wanted to be closer to her. Plus, two of my Mom's brothers were living out there too. My Mom's boyfriend had flown out there ahead of us and got us an apartment in a large complex with a pool in between each building. It was summer so it was very hot. Our apartment had one bedroom and there was my Mom, her boyfriend, my brother, and myself. My brother and I were not too happy with this arrangement at all. We both spent a lot of time that summer at my sister's apartment and I looked after my niece a lot. I was only nine at the time, but they trusted me to watch her.

I was to start school there in the fall. But our stay in Las Vegas was cut short because my Mom's boyfriend got very violent with my Mom and pretty much left her for dead. Next thing I know, my Mom, brother, and myself are on a plane back to our family home. We weren't home but a few weeks when Mom told us she couldn't afford the house and we had to sell it. We were moving back to Grams again. What a great way to spend your summer, right?

I began sixth grade back in the original school system I had started in back in kindergarten. You can imagine by age ten what my self-esteem was like?

I practically lived upstairs in my Aunt's apartment. They didn't drink, they always had food, and I had a cousin who was the same age as me to hang around with. I only went down to our apartment to sleep at night. My brother was still heavily into drugs and got in trouble constantly, but we were still very close.

With practically no supervision going into Junior High, I had already started smoking and I tried my first drink by age 12. Life was pretty much a big party for me. My grades were terrible, I was never home, and in my freshman year of high school, I missed 80 days out of 180. I failed all my classes one term and was almost held back. I made it to sophomore year and the school decided to call in my Dad because they were concerned about me. I remember walking by the guidance office and seeing my Dad and my stepmom in there. I was so angry. "Why are you here? I'm doing just fine without you," I thought to myself.

My Mom used to tell me stories about my Dad. That he didn't want to pay child support. That he spent all his money on his wife. We were poor and he had plenty of money. I'm sure you can imagine what this did for my inner story about financial abundance. Later, I did find out his side and it was more like he didn't want to give my Mom money because she would spend it on alcohol instead of me.

Not too long after this, my brother went to rehab for the third time. I was completely out of control and something needed to change. I will go into more details on why I left later in the book, but one thing I knew at this point, I had to get out of there if I was ever going to make it in life. At 15 years old, I went to live with my Dad. I started to do better in school, but I was still no angel.

My senior year in high school, I used to cruise the back roads to school. I would get high before I went in. My dad had bought an old Mercedes Benz and gifted it to me when I got my license. One day I was cruising when I heard this voice say, "You're going to get in an accident. You need to wear your seatbelt." I ignored it, writing it off as a guilty conscience. On May 11th, 1990, I woke up late for school. I asked my dad to sign a note and I took my sweet time getting ready. I rolled a fat joint, got in my car, and took the back way to school. As I was putting out the joint in my ashtray, I took my eyes off of the road. I looked up and all I saw was this huge tree, "BOOM." I slammed into the tree, dead on, and I wasn't wearing my seatbelt. I woke up in my car and tried to get out of the door, but it was jammed shut. The car was still in drive. I crawled over to the passenger side and got out and started walking. I was on a back road where there are not very many houses around. I realized I was hurting really badly and needed help. Dizziness consumed me as I fell in the middle of the road. I forced myself back up and saw a car driving towards me. This lady (an angel), told me to get in her car. She drove to the police station. I was in bad shape. My stomach hurt so badly, and I couldn't see anything but white outlines of the trees in front of me. The ambulance arrived, they placed me on a stretcher, and I was on my way to the hospital. I could hear them calling my dad over the radio while we were en route. I was petrified that he was going to be so disappointed in me. I had totaled my car. In the ER, I remember the whole ordeal. The doctors, my Dad coming in, and being told I need surgery.

When I woke up from surgery. I found out I lacerated my liver with the impact of the steering wheel. I was in a ton of pain. I had 30 staples all the way down my stomach from the surgery. At 17 years old, this was a huge blow. I remember thinking, now I'm going to have this huge, blotchy scar down my entire stomach for the rest of my life. How was I supposed to graduate in a few weeks?

After a week in the hospital recovering, I was able to go home. It was hard to go back to living after that. Even just getting in the car on the way home from the hospital made my blood run cold. I had a ton of work to make up at school, but I pressed on. I returned to school one week before graduation and spoke with all of my teachers. We worked out grades and on June 3rd I graduated with my class, only by a miracle. This was the first time I thought God must want me here for a reason.

At the time, I had a boyfriend, who was 12 years older than me. He actually went to school with my sisters. No one in my family could understand why I was with him. But he was sober when we met, and he took good care of me. He was in construction and lived in a house taking care of his elderly Dad. We were just friends for a long time, but something changed after I graduated high school and we became more serious. After I moved in, he started to drink again and that progressed into doing drugs. I had stopped drinking around age 16 because I poisoned myself enough one night with a bottle of Southern Comfort and realized I couldn't keep doing that to myself. I stayed with him, hoping it would stop just as abruptly as it started. It didn't. I found myself pregnant at age 20 and with a man who never wanted to have children. I wasn't giving up my baby and our relationship really started to go downhill from there. I had to be responsible and be a good Mom for our son but my boyfriend was drifting farther and farther into his addiction. At age 23, I found myself pregnant again with our second child and within a year of my daughter being born, I was a single mother. I left him because of his addiction. I did not want my kids to grow up like I did.

I ended up meeting a man soon after who I fell in love with. We had a long-distance relationship for many years before the kids and I moved in with him and his parents in their family home. We got married when the kids were 8 and 10 and I thought life was going to finally be happy and stable.

As it turns out, not so much. My fantasy life with my loving husband in a nice house with a great school system for my kids turned into a power struggle between his parents and myself over how I should be raising my kids. I had my way and they had their opinions of my way. I tried to do things their way but found my kids were starting to resent me for it. In order to save my relationship with my kids, we moved out of the house into an apartment. My husband was torn and chose to stay at the house with his parents instead of moving with me and the kids. So, I lost my husband, who was my best friend, and was a single Mom once again with an 11- and 13-year-old.

When I was looking for a place for us to go, I chose to move back to the town where my Gram lived. I guess it's where you could say I "grew up." It was where I was most comfortable and knew I would have some support from family and friends. My Mom had passed at this point, but I knew a lot of people there. I was working full-time and able to support my kids, but I was not happy, to say the least.

At 39 years old, I found myself alone, separated, and raising two teenagers. All my thoughts were depictions of anxiety, poverty, and hopeless despair. I knew there was more to my life than this, but I felt so stuck in a rut and barely capable of surviving.

One night I was speaking with my oldest sister and I shared how I was feeling. She put me on hold and when she returned, she started reading me this book, *You Can Heal Your Life* by Louise Hay. I listened intently to her talk about how a thought is just a thought, and a thought can be changed. Inspired, I ordered the book after our call and read the entire thing that same night. I discovered the power of positivity and the law of attraction. The mere sentence, "A thought is just a thought, and a thought can be changed" was such a profound revelation for me. Through learning about metaphysical teachings, I realized that the voice I heard at 17 telling me to wear my seatbelt was my connection with the universe, or God, if you will.

It was such a fascination for me.] I could start to see how much more there is to life than just what we are on this physical plane in our day to day lives. I started learning all I can about spirituality, angels, and even the Bible. I started to pay attention to my thoughts, to how I'm speaking, to how I act, and began to turn my negatives into positives. I started to tell myself a different story: I am good enough, I am smart enough, and ,most of all, I believe in myself. Things started to change little by little. I felt really good instead of exhausted and drained. I became unstoppable in my achievements. For once, I felt hope for my future.

I decided to go back to college. It was a promise I made to myself way back when. I wanted to be a good role model for my kids and show them that it's never too late to accomplish anything you set your mind to. I decided to enroll at the University of Phoenix and worked for over two years to get my Bachelor of Science degree in IT for Web Development. It wasn't easy raising two teens, working full-time, and taking classes in the evenings at home. I completed 24 classes in just two and a half years and was able to finally move out of the mail center after ten years, and into the software group, where I am currently an SQA Engineer.

Although I was doing well, I was concerned about one of my kids. I could see the same teenage patterns from when I was their age creeping in with the party scene, grades dropping, and not wanting to listen to any advice from Mom. Not one ounce of my being as a parent wanted my children to endure addiction. I educated them about it openly and they saw their Grammy sick before she passed. They heard plenty of stories of their Uncle Dan and how messed up he is. I did the best I could, but when they say "it runs in the family" they are correct. My family is riddled with addiction and it has no preference over who it affects. I'd like to keep most of my son's journey private, but I will get into it a bit more later as

I feel sharing my story will help others and is necessary.

I know that was a lot, and I have left out many details of this journey I call life, but the main takeaway for anyone reading this is that for a little girl who started life in an uphill climb from the start, I never gave up. It took me 40 years to learn that I am beautiful, smart, courageous, and worth loving. My goal is to help you begin your healing journey as I share more in depth about how I was able to heal mentally, physically, and spiritually and show you some examples of how you can start to do the same.

My destiny is now set to share what I've learned. To inspire others, and to teach them that there is more to life than what you see through your eyes. We all have a soul destiny inside of us. If we can just quiet our minds and follow our hearts, we will soon discover our own destinies and move towards greatness. This journey hasn't been easy. I didn't just wake up one day and things were magical. I'm still here on this earth with all the drama, tragedy, and disruption, but I don't see most of it.

I am now making a difference by helping those who face family addiction. We all have choices in life.

I've made some bad and some good. We are not perfect, nor should we be. We are meant to expand and grow, each of us, in our own ways. Our world is a gift and we can open that gift every day. I'm grateful I went through my struggles and I know there will be more. It's ok though, because with my inner guidance, I will persevere.

The most important lesson I learned is to come from a place of service and not to focus on the material world. Now I'm able to share my lessons and help others design their destiny, to discover their true desires.

In a sense I self-healed through trial and error. My core belief when I hear excuses is, "if I can do it after all I've been through anyone can do it." I'd like that anyone to be you. I've provided some examples and steps to begin your journey to joy and look forward to serving you with more wisdom if you so desire.

Chapter 1. When is Enough Enough, and How Do We Begin to Change it?

"Addiction breaks all the bonds, hearts, and all the rules"
Sandy Swenson

Before we begin....

In the Introduction, I mentioned that I self-healed my past traumas and insecurities through finding what I call spirituality, or the universe. Some people call it God. I do believe in God, but have learned that when you are explaining or talking about a higher power it's best to generalize it to something almost anyone can relate to. So please note that when I'm speaking about the universe or source you can replace that with whichever term you are most comfortable with. If you don't believe in anything that's okay, but I'll ask you to keep an open mind throughout because how I got to where I am was not just my will to survive and grow. I've had guidance along the way, and I think you will see that in this book.

Another quick note: I don't personally care for the word "addict." These are our loved ones, who happen to have an issue with addiction, but they themselves are not addiction, they are spiritual beings who are "in there" somewhere, lost, with a brain that is sick and craving more of what it knows best. For our loved one's sake, I will be replacing the word "addict" with "loved one" throughout these chapters.

From my experience, I believe most people in addiction have an underlying issue causing them to turn to alcohol or drugs to cope. Some are injuries and some are mental illness issues, but it all starts with some type of pain, physical or mental. I don't feel they should be labeled so harshly for this reason.

It's Hard to Admit Someone You Love Has an Addiction

I'm going to jump right into the heart of it. Living with addiction is hard! It's hard to talk about, admit to ourselves and others, and it consumes our everyday life if we let it. We, as codependents, often feel like we need to hide it from others. We feel embarrassed to admit that our husband, wife, parent, friend, or even our own child has an issue with addiction.

In Being Honest with Yourself

Do you feel like you just can't admit to yourself or someone else your loved one is living in addiction? Ask yourself why? Is it just too hard to say the words because it hurts too much? Maybe you feel like somehow it is your fault?

    I can relate. When I was growing up, I couldn't really bring friends over to my house because I never knew what shape my Mom would be in. She spent most of the day in bed so it's a little hard to explain to your friends that she was up all night drinking and that's why at 2 o'clock in the afternoon, she's asleep in a dark room instead of working or spending time with me. So, I just avoided having friends come over instead.

    Please don't get me wrong, as with all of our loved ones in addiction, my Mom was an amazing person. She was very loving and very caring. I learned a lot of my better qualities from her. She would give the shirt off her back to anyone. She was popular. Everyone loved Gail. She was my Mom, and through everything we went through, I loved her more than I could ever express. She passed away at age 61 in 2004. Her body had had enough of the alcohol and we had that fateful day where the doctors told my sisters and I, "I'm sorry there is nothing more we can do for her."

    If you can relate to the questions above, I want you to know that I was there too, on so many levels. And now I'm here to help you recognize some of the thought patterns we go through when we have a loved one in addiction. My goal is to help you change the way you feel, think, and react to the problems your loved ones in addiction bring into your life. I've learned through talking with others who face family addiction that we all have the same story, different person. When we can accept that we are not alone on this journey, it becomes easier to talk about with others and by talking about it and sharing our experiences, we begin to heal.

    I want to help you to recognize the patterns of codependency and how to break free so you can give yourself permission to live your life again, even if your loved one is not in recovery. I can't make your loved one's addiction go away, but I can provide you with some tools to find your joy inside again.

When is enough, enough?

I see many people in the thick of coping with their loved one's addiction ask this: How do I know when enough is enough with my loved one?

My answer to this is a question: are you enjoying the experiences you are living right now? Here are my thoughts: You will begin to know when enough is enough when you finally admit to yourself that your loved one has a problem. Once you can admit to yourself that your loved one has a problem, you may find that you seek answers about why they are doing this. You will see more clearly that you have become tired of the lies, tired of them asking for money or help, or even stealing from you to feed their addiction. It's hard, but at some point, we become tired of feeling weak and giving in to them, and we begin to realize that something has to change. Only when we can admit that our loved one has a problem, we begin to search for the answers.

My First "Enough is Enough" Experience (Parent in Addiction)

When I was 15, things were pretty out of control. I was not in a good place mentally and my brother was doing more partying and getting into more trouble than anyone ever should. For all three of us, including my Mom, life was pretty much a mess. I remember that it was cold and my brother and I were sitting in the kitchen talking about getting my Mom some help. She had locked herself in her room with a closet full of booze and all she did was sleep and drink for days. She even fell asleep with a cigarette and caught her mattress on fire one night. So we decided to take action to get her help. We tried to force her into the car to bring her to rehab when she came out to go to the bathroom. Things got really ugly. She didn't want to go, and ran back into her room and locked the door. My brother smashed in the bedroom door and tried to drag her out again. Needless to say, he was hurting her because she was so frail. I was so full of anxiety as I watched them struggle. I hated to see her like this. Our aunt (her sister) lived next door, heard the commotion, and, of course, took my Mom's side. She called the police and told them that my brother and I didn't live there, and we were only there to cause trouble. I was so angry with her. Here we were trying to save our Mom, and my aunt was trying to protect her from us. Funny how family works.

The police advised us to let it go for the night, and to go to the courthouse to get a summons issued for her to go to treatment. The next day, my sister, brother, and myself did just that. We got a summons for the police to deliver so they could take her to rehab. Back then in small towns, people were pretty tight. The sergeant on duty knew my Mom and refused to deliver the summons. I'm not sure if they can do that, but this one did.

On that day, December 24th, I decided to get out of there and move in with my Dad. I called my sister and packed my things in trash bags. She came and picked me up and I left my Mom. I needed to do what was best for me and staying in that house, living the way we were, was not what I needed. I was smoking and drinking myself. I never went to school and I didn't care much about anything but partying. I knew at that point that I wouldn't make it in life if I didn't take the decision to put myself first and do what was best for me.

On Christmas Day, I got a call from my sister saying that my Mom had gone into rehab. My uncle had picked her up. She wouldn't allow any of her kids to see her while she was in there. I can remember how much that hurt. But she only stayed a week before she was home again.

I learned that I couldn't save her at an early age, but I also learned that I couldn't live there anymore and watch her die. It was one of the toughest decisions I've ever made, but one I will never regret. I stayed as long as I could because I thought she needed me but what she really needed was to find herself and love herself enough to get sober and heal. Back then, we didn't know as much about addiction as we do today and she was too proud to ask for help.

That feeling of not being able to help her haunted me for a long time, but I had to save myself. Today I've done the work to heal from this hurt. I've empowered myself to not be powerless. I decided to live my life on purpose, knowing she would be proud of me.

Most of us think that we are stuck on this journey of living with a loved one in addiction. We feel like we can't throw our loved ones out, or leave ourselves, because they wouldn't survive without our help. But on the other hand, you're here reading this book because you are tired of your loved one's addiction and you just want it to stop. You've tried talking to them about it. You've tried to get them help and, if they weren't ready, it failed. You've bailed them out time and time again, and you're just tired. This is when it's time to realize that you are powerless and enough is enough. When you feel the most despair and hopelessness, this is where true healing begins. This is where the action of realizing that you are important ,and you and your family need you to be courageous and strong so you can begin to heal.

My Second "Enough is Enough" Experience (Partner in Addiction)

I found myself faced with these feelings again when I was living with my children's father. When my children were almost one and three years old, his behavior was getting ugly. He was drinking, doing drugs, and couldn't hold a job to save his life. I was supporting our family and raising our kids alone. One night, sitting in the kitchen at dinner, my son wanted some juice. I told him he could get it out of the fridge and bring it to me. All excited to be a big helper, D went to the fridge and brought me the juice. When my ex saw this, he started to scream at me. Something to the effect of "why are you letting a two-year-old open the fridge and get the juice?" This was a true aha moment for me. Something just triggered and brought me back to my childhood with my Mom's boyfriend. At that moment, I refused to raise my kids the way I grew up. I started the wheels in motion for the kids and myself to get away from him as soon as possible. There was no way I was going to raise them like that. Screaming about a two-year-old getting juice out of the fridge, really?

    Thanks to the support of my Dad and my middle sister, I was able to leave and get an apartment in the next town over shortly after that. Becoming a single parent at 24 was not easy, but I have no regrets about leaving him. It was hard to pick up and leave my two beautiful dogs behind, but just the thought of having my children continue to grow up around a raging alcoholic who flies off the handle over the little things was the final straw to get me to take action and leave. Sounds easy right? Believe me, I know it's not as easy as I make it sound. Had I not grown up with addiction, it may not have been so easy, but if you and your family are in a situation where your loved one is out of control, it's time to really look at who you want to become in this life and where you want to go. And most importantly what is it costing you to keep living like this? Think about the impression you want for your children growing up, if you have children. Even if you don't have children, think about what you want for you.

If you've tried to help your loved one and they are not on the same page, then it's time to make a change. Not to start thinking about making a change, but to actually take action. I'm here to tell you that's it's okay if you decide to make them leave or to leave yourself. If it's your husband or wife who is addicted, it's ok to consider getting a divorce. Even though you love them, you need to love yourself more.

Let me ask you this, do you want to spend the rest of your marriage watching them hurt themselves and damage your family, or do you want to live your life again and begin to heal?

We struggle with feelings of abandonment and giving up on them, but what are they doing for you right now? Why should you feel this way when they do not?

It is the hardest thing in the world to say to a loved one, "home is not an option," but in order for you to begin to hea,l you need to trust in your inner strength. For your own healing, if your situation feels that bad, you may need to let your loved one know that "home is not an option anymore."

As I Reflect On My Time As a Child:

As a child, I had to cope with my Mom as a dysfunctional alcoholic and my Dad living so far away. As a little girl, I only saw him when he could pick me up for a weekend, here or there. I lived in an environment with constant parties and drinking where I didn't have a voice to say when enough was enough. I was dragged into bars after school or I came home to an empty house to fend for myself. I lay in my bed at night listening to my Mom and her boyfriend scream at each other with tears streaming down my face silently saying, "just stop, just stop." One night, he was hurting my Mom. I ran into the room and tried to stop him. He scooped me up and held me over his head, shaking me, telling me to stay out of it. I was only eight years old. Fearless and tired of it all, I didn't care how much bigger than me he was. He wasn't going to hurt my Mom. I had no choice but to live with it because no one knew how much it was really hurting me. I was too scared to tell my Dad because I didn't want to get my Mom in trouble. I just kept it all inside and always felt so alone.

I share this for the first time because you need to be the voice for your family and do your best to heal and find joy again so you can have the peace and happiness you deserve.

I want to reiterate: it is okay to put yourself first and to be courageous enough to make these changes regardless of who it is in your family who is addicted, because this is about your life. This is about you! *You deserve to be happy.*

My Third Enough is Enough Experience (Sibling in Addiction)

As a brother or a sister, we feel loyalty to our siblings. It can be a love/hate relationship at times, but what are siblings for? When we have a sibling in addiction, we can also take on the role of codependent with them. As teens, we may cover for them when they stay out past curfew or lie to our parents for them if they are out partying. Sometimes we party right along with them. But sometimes they take that wrong path and end up in addiction and when they keep asking us to bail them out we find ourselves at a crossroad between wanting to help them and wanting them to save themselves. It's okay to tell your sibling "no." It's okay to let someone know if you think they have a problem. You could be saving their life.

    I shared earlier that our family was split up in the divorce. My sisters went with my Dad and my brother and I stayed with my Mom. I was loyal to him, and he and I had a really special relationship. As we got older, he got shuffled back and forth between our parents because he was the "trouble child." He was doing all kinds of drugs as a pre-teen and by the time he was an adult, I can't even tell you all the stories of what he did and put both my parents through. If you have a sibling in addiction you can probably just imagine what life was like watching the person you look up to the most destroy themselves.

As adults, he went his way and I went mine, but we have always stayed in touch. My Dad tended to help him all the time, enabling him when he called with a story about how bad his life was. It was guilt driven. He tried to help my brother over the years but nothing he did worked, so giving him money was his way of coping. When my Dad passed away in 2014, my brother's "safety net" with money was gone. He went downhill fast in his addiction and today he looks like a 70-year old-man in a 50-something body.

In 2019, due to a traumatic event in my brother's life, I had him come up north to stay with me. It's a long story, but he was hooked on heroin and is a severe alcoholic. He was very sick and called me for money daily. I knew that throwing money at him was not a long-term solution, so I put him on a bus to be with me instead.

When he first arrived, I was able to help him detox from heroin, but I was not able to convince him to stop drinking. I was close, but it has such a grip on him that sadly I've come to realize he will never stop drinking until his body has had enough. I pray for him and keep my light shining in my heart for Daniel.

I could go into so much more detail about how this all came about, but I want to keep the point of this story focused on the effects his coming to stay had on me because I made the decision to let someone in addiction back into my life.

The first part of the year, I was in my happy place (I call it my bubble). I was doing my inner work and feeling good about myself. As the year went on, I found myself becoming more and more unhappy living with his behaviors. I was trying to change him, and I know better, but the codependent in me wanted to try. On a daily basis, he listened to loud music to drown out his voices in his head. I prefer a quiet, serene environment. I tolerated the music because I knew it was helping him, but it wasn't helping me. He drank 18 beers a day, so there were constant beer cans in my sink and recycling. I rarely drink myself, so having to tolerate seeing him wake up and crack a beer went against everything in my being. But hey, at least he wasn't using heroin, this is how I justified it. I tried daily to plant seeds and to give him advice, but it definitely didn't penetrate.

As time went on, I found myself screaming at him and nothing he did, right or wrong, was good enough for me. I was miserable and really started to feel hatred towards him for my own feelings and actions. Another key lesson I've learned is that you are responsible for how you feel and no one else is. Yet every time I'd walk through my front door and that music was blaring, I would fill with rage and just want him gone.

I love my brother more than anything, but I couldn't stand another minute with him living in my house. We both knew it wasn't working and came to the conclusion that he needed to leave. He was unhappy living up here with me because he can't drive and I started to say no to things he wanted or needed so he went back to what he knew best, struggling and being surrounded by people who live the same lifestyle he knows best.

I have to admit that I sighed a sigh of relief once he was gone (love you brother) but I needed desperately to get back to who I was yet again. But even though I was relieved, I found that I had crept back so far into who I used to be in that one year with him that I didn't even know how to stop being angry and frustrated. I was so very angry at myself for losing the person I worked so hard to be before he came to live with me. The me I had worked so hard to become was gone. I didn't even know where to start again, yet I knew I had to begin somewhere. Maybe you can relate?

When It's Your Child in Addiction

If it's your child who faces addiction, as a Mom who's also been there, I'm here to say it's okay to legally force them to get help if they are under the age of 18 if you think they have an issue. I highly recommend this, because once they turn 18 you lose your voice in their medical and legal matters. I went through the nightmares with HIPA here in the US, trying to get my son help because he was over 18, and I am here to say that even though they are still "your" child, you have zero say in the eyes of the law.

If you have a child under 18 and they are living with you and you feel they need help, don't hesitate. They will forgive you and maybe even thank you later if

they find their way to recovery (if you need info on sectioning a loved one, laws are different in every state in the US, but here is some info from MA on section 35 as a guideline for getting started:
https://www.mass.gov/section-35)

    I say all this because I wrote off my son's party habits when he was younger as just teen behavior. As he got to his early 20s, I learned that I really needed to take his partying seriously sooner due to events I will share later in the book, so, from a Mom who has learned the hard way, please don't wait to get them help if you have a child who appears to be using any form of self-medicating substances.

    If you have tried to help and were not successful, please don't ever give up on them. I talk a lot about letting go and healing yourself through this journey, but when it is your child, no matter how old they are, it can feel hopeless and lonely. Keep your light shining for them and if it's bright enough, maybe they will see it and start to shine theirs too.

Getting Out of a State of Denial

When we are in a state of denial about our loved one's addiction, we are not serving ourselves or others on the highest level. We are carrying lies around with us, hiding from the truth. These lies are heavy and it's time to put them down. It's time to let them go. Your loved one's addiction is their path to travel. Your path is to admit they have a problem and to figure out how to love yourself enough to heal the hurt.

    I remember as an adult listening to my Mom lie about her drinking. By this time, I had long ago accepted that she was an alcoholic and I couldn't change her. I knew she was still drinking, but ever since I left when I was 15, she had decided that she needed to pretend she didn't drink anymore when she was around me. She would call me to ask me to bring her to the store. My one rule was: "I will take you anywhere but don't ask me to go to the liquor store for you." She would reply, "Oh sure, I don't drink anymore so we can just go to the grocery store." She didn't need me to go to the liquor store anyways because she had my uncle for that. Even though I had come to terms with her alcoholism, she somehow felt that she needed to hide it from me so I would continue to have a relationship with her. It was always in the back of her mind that had I left her as a teen because of her drinking so she felt she needed to cover for herself around me. I loved my Mom regardless of her drinking, but admitting to myself that I was powerless over it helped me to be free from it. It was important to me to be able to continue to have a relationship with her regardless of who and what she was. She never admitted it to herself although I know that deep down she knew. It's hard to admit your faults but we all have them and wanting to accept that and learn from it is the key to having a happier, more stable life.

Something to Think About:

You were given this life and although you care deeply about your loved one, it's up to you to control *your* destiny, not theirs. I've learned that we are all born to discover and reach our own destinies. We each have a path in life, and we all experience our own lessons, bumps, pleasures, and achievements on this path. Think about it, life in itself is a miracle. Take a moment and look around you, how did you arrive where you are now? Have you stopped recently and looked at the sky? When was the last time you caught a sunrise or a sunset? Or just stopped for a moment and looked around at the beauty of our planet, the stars, the clouds, or the moon? Our universe is so mystifying and beautiful and you are so caught up in your loved one's addiction that you are missing your own destiny.

When we live with family addiction instead of focusing on ourselves and who we want to become, we see dark days, despair, and depression. We are unhappy, sad, and scared. It's not fair. We are meant to feel love, happiness and joy and so, one last time, I'll ask you, when is enough enough?

I've seen cases where parents have said enough is enough and their loved one has lost their battle, but I've also seen many cases where a loved one finds their path to recovery because their family or friends loved themselves enough to say, "I'm important too, and I'm choosing happiness over addiction, love over fear, and acceptance over denial." Once you can do this, you will begin to trust in your decisions about your path in your loved one's addiction and begin to heal.

Chapter 2. Breaking the Cycle of Codependency

"There is great change to be experienced once you learn the power of letting go. Stop allowing anyone or anything to control, limit, repress, or discourage you from being your true self! Today is YOURS to shape - own it - break free from people and things that poison or dilute your spirit." Steve Maraboli, *Unapologetically You: Reflections on Life and the Human Experience*

What Codependency Is and How It Affects You

According to Melody Beattie in her book, *Codependent No More: How to Stop Controlling Others and Start Caring For Yourself*, "A Codependent person is one who has let another person's behavior affect him or her and who is obsessed with controlling that person's behavior."

When we take on the role of codependent, we get so wrapped up in what our loved one is doing that we often put ourselves last. We may even forget to eat, or the opposite, and eat more because of the stress of worrying about what they are doing or where they are or what will happen next. When you try to constantly fix or protect your loved one, it feels so time consuming and exhausting, doesn't it? Have you forgotten what it is you like to do? Do you still work at your hobbies or are they shoved in a corner in your mind somewhere, a distant memory of what your life used to be like?

Welcome to Codependency

As Codependents we worry so much about everybody else that when we don't have someone or something to worry about, we don't know what to do with ourselves. We never worry about ourselves though, do we? We don't even realize that this is not normal and that we are living a life ruled by other people's behaviors.

See if you can relate to these things:

- Taking on our loved one's problems as if they are our own.
- Covering for their poor choices to protect them from the judgement of others.
- Going above and beyond to please everyone because you feel like you have to.
- Not feeling worthy of love or compliments from others
- Neglecting your own needs because you put everyone else first.

A strong trait in codependency is people pleasing. We want to do and be everything for everyone. It becomes part of our nature to want to do it all, but we can't. Now, if you're like me, you might be offended by the last part of that sentence. "You can't" do something. I know how it feels to me, even today, when someone tells me I can't do something. My reaction tends to be, "oh yeah, watch me!" This inner feeling is something I am consciously aware of and have to practice letting go of.

For your sake, it's time to stop saying "yes" when you want to say "no." Just practice saying "no" when you don't want to do something. It doesn't always have to be about your loved one in addiction either. If you are doing this at home, you're probably doing it in other relationships as well. Just say "no" when it goes against your inner guidance. It will be okay. The person might be upset with you, but, if they are, that's their problem, not yours. You have to start setting boundaries for yourself so you can focus on the most important thing – you. We will talk more about boundaries in the next chapter.

Another eye opener for me as I started to study codependent traits were these questions: When is the last time you let someone do something for you when they offered? When was the last time you asked someone for help? I find it so hard when someone says, "oh, let me do that for you." I get upset and tell them, "I got this, but thank you anyway." I struggle with letting people do things for me or asking for help. On so many occasions in my life, I chose not to learn or do something because I didn't want to ask for help. I would feel embarrassed, like I was some helpless child or something, or, at least, I used to. Part of the work of healing from codependency is letting others do things for you when they offer or accepting a compliment when it is given. It takes practice and awareness of your feelings at the time. I know our loved ones in addiction never offer us help, and we often state how selfish they are, but I'm talking about other instances with other people in your daily life. What do you say when someone tells you they like your hair or the shoes you have on? Do you say, "oh my hair is a mess today, or oh those are so old"? Or do you just reply, "Thank You" and accept the compliment? I know that in the past I would counter whatever compliment someone gave me and turn it into something that put me down. Do you do this too?

These are just a few examples of how living with a loved one in addiction can create codependent behaviors that we carry with us, not realizing that we are limiting ourselves. We need to stop living life this way and start living our lives on purpose, for ourselves.

How to begin the healing process

I would never kid you and say that when you use the techniques I teach you in this book, you will free from your loved one's addiction or the learned habits we inherit from the experience. We are never free from it completely. We experience so much trauma and pain that even if our loved ones are in recovery, there is always a sense of lack of trust or self-doubt that creeps in at random times and becomes the norm in our thinking.

Trust is hard to come by in addiction, so we constantly think our loved ones are up to no good or are lying to us, well, because "the only time someone in addiction is lying, is every time their lips are moving!" Or we do the opposite, and start questioning our own judgements when we feel like something is off. Our loved ones in addiction do a good job of convincing us that it's not them and that it's our fault when we question their behaviors. Before we know it, we don't know what to believe anymore. The minute you let your guard down and believe what they say, they will disappoint you. If you can relate to this then it is time for you to do the work to let them go and break your codependent patterns for good.

Nothing changes if we don't create change. Your loved one is comfortable and certainly isn't going to just stop their behavior without becoming uncomfortable. By giving them no option and taking back control of your life, you are actually helping them, even if it feels like the worst thing you could ever do.

"God grant me the serenity to accept the things I cannot change, the courage to change the things I can, and the wisdom to know the difference." Reinhold Niebuhr

Letting go is a part of healing. There's a Zen proverb I like to use, "Let Go or Be Dragged." We need to grow and evolve as humans and being in a codependent relationship stops us from doing just that. All of our focus goes on our loved ones. We don't remember who we are anymore, and before we know it, years have passed, and we've missed out on so much. It's time now to get back to you!

Taking the next steps

The first step in healing is to admit that you are powerless over your loved one's addiction, which is true, but you do have a choice and that next step is to empower yourself. It starts with accepting the fact that the only one who can help your loved one, is your loved one. If you haven't yet come to terms with the fact that you can't help your loved one, then you probably want to slam this book shut and tell me to go to hell! But please don't. Instead, take a deep breath and stay right here with me where it's hard for a moment, it will get easier.

The good news is that any recovering loved one will tell you that when their family finally said "enough is enough," it was the best thing that ever happened to them. Now, this may be hard to believe from your point of view but what you need to remember is that you are important too and you deserve a life filled with peace and happiness. Most loved ones who hit bottom and find recovery tell stories of how their families disowned them and then go on to say how good this was for them.

By doing the work to strengthen your vision about your own life and how it could really be instead of what it is right now, you will be helping them too. Because you can stand up and say, "enough is enough," it gives them no choice but to go about their battle on their own. They are very resourceful, and just because you stop helping them or living the life they are dictating through their behaviors, it doesn't make you a bad person. It shows that you care enough about yourself and them to make the changes you need to make so that you can begin to heal.

Remember, this is about you. You are here for you. Yes, your loved one is a big part of your life, but you are also here because of them. And if you are here, you are feeling hurt, helpless, defenseless, tired, sad, mad, and fed up with being lied to, stolen from, and cheated out of peace and harmony. You want this to end and you have tried to stop it, but you can't. Here is your other option: put fear aside, empower yourself to heal, and move forward on your path towards living in happiness and joy.

You are not alone on this journey. There are so many of us who walk family addiction with you. Surround yourself with others who know the same story and who also have a strong desire to heal, to live their own lives free of anxiety, worry, hurt, and depression. Decide today to let go and be free!

Now That You've Decided to Let Go

"When we let go of our reactions and detach from other people's moods, actions, and words, we take back our power. Instead of reactors, we become self-determined actors in our lives. We take charge of ourselves and decide how we act in that moment and every moment, skyrocketing our self-esteem." Darlene Lancer, *Codependency for Dummies*

Remember that your loved one needs you more than you need their behavior. Becoming strong starts with educating yourself in addiction and the effects it has on you as a codependent. As a reminder from the previous section, what was the second step in healing? **Deciding that you are empowered.**

Honestly, I can say that it took me 40 years to come to terms with how living with the effects of my family's addiction has altered my behavior and my path in life. I'm grateful for all the lessons because they made me who I am today, but it took a lot of inner work to start to heal.

I'm sharing some of what I've learned with you so you too can begin to heal and move forward sooner than later. I want you to be the main focus throughout these chapters because this is your time, and it's time to live a happy, joy-filled life. Even though much of what I relay to you is about my life, my hope is there is a story or two you can relate to your own experiences.

Recognizing and Changing the Patterns

As a child in school, I didn't try hard to get good grades because I didn't think I was smart enough. As a teen, I turned to smoking and drinking by the age of 12 or 13 due to lack of discipline. Because my Mom was so unhealthy and dysfunctional from her drinking, I acted like I could do whatever I wanted, and, I assure you, none of it was good or positive except my love for playing sports. Even after I left my Mom's at 15 because I had had enough and had a more stable life living at my Dad's, I still didn't do the healing work. I worked on myself a little to stay in school and to stop drinking but by continuing the patterns I had learned over the years, the results continued to show up in my life. I didn't finish college as a young adult and ended up pregnant with my first child at age 20. Of course, I chose what I knew best in a man – an alcoholic and drug addict –

which resulted in becoming a single Mom of two by age 24 before I finally decided enough was enough for my children's sake. But I still didn't do the healing work and the patterns continued.

The point is that when we are living with a loved one in addiction, we don't see the big picture. We are doing what we think is best for both them and ourselves at the time, and we miss out on our own true potential. You are here because you want something more. You want to disrupt the patterns keeping you from your joy, and that's a good start. Have you decided that you've hit your rock bottom and it's time to start to climb now?

How I Found My Rock Bottom and Started to Heal

As the years went on ,I struggled to raise my kids financially and mentally. I learned a lot about myself through all these challenges though. When I turned 39, I started to recognize how negative my thoughts always were. I was living in constant fear, to the point where I would have severe panic attacks every time my kids walked out the door without me. I constantly thought about terrible things happening to them. I couldn't even stand to hear myself talk anymore. I couldn't say anything nice about anything or anyone.

Once I decided to put in the work to heal, I was able to recognize the thoughts and patterns I was living in. I learned how to change them so I could live a more positive, fulfilling lifestyle beyond my loved ones' addictions. I discovered that the way I was viewing myself, and how I kept repeating codependent patterns, was due to the damage caused by growing up with addiction. I was able to start exercising again and journal and just do things I love without worrying about what anyone else was doing.

I even discovered that my children's Dad's underlying issues were with mental health, and that drinking and drugs were a way to cover the fear and hurt he endured when his mother passed away from cancer at an early age.

How You Too Can Change Your Patterns

When you can learn to focus on the positive outcome you want and not the negative things in front of you, things will start to change. Even if you can't see it right now, try to start paying attention to your thoughts and, if they are negative, shift your focus to better thoughts. Just this little practice every day will create change for the better.

In coaching my clients, I begin them on the journey of healing by recognizing their inner story and how it is keeping them from their joy. I shift their mindset to recognize how the story they are telling themselves and others is keeping them stuck. I take them through changing their story to one of a courageous survivor, who does not carry the label of codependency, but is a strong, loving, and caring person who finds happiness through helping others and in turn helping themselves.

I want to give this gift to you now. Below is an exercise where you can start to capture your negative story and change it to a new story full of everything you desire. I hope you will take the time right now to embark on this journey with me.

Happy Story Exercise

Get yourself a notebook and a pen. Yes, a notebook and a pen, not your phone or computer. Writing is healing. Letting your thoughts flow through the pen takes them out of your head and aids in letting them go.

Stay with me now...

I want you to think about your life as it is right now (I call this your inner story). You know your story, the one you tell everyone about how things aren't as good as they could be and how you wish things were different.

What is the story you are telling yourself on a daily basis? Make a list of the thoughts that play over and over in your head. I want you to keep your notebook with you throughout your day. Pay attention to what you are thinking about and, when you recognize that you are running your negative story, capture the thoughts in your notebook. Do this for a few days until you can consciously recognize them when they come up.

After a few days of writing down what comes up for you on a daily basis, I want you to review it and ask yourself: Is this really who you are? Is this really how things are? If you believe it, then it must be real, right?

The answer is no. These thoughts seem real because you are giving your attention to them. What if every time you recognize a negative thought, you stop it in its tracks and replace it with something new? What if you start to disrupt your story and change it to something better? Would it then become real?

The answer here is yes. The reason is because we are what we give our attention to. It's that simple. If you start to change your story and design your life in your mind the way you want it to be, you will see it start to change. It may sound far-fetched, but I'm asking you to try. Do this exercise and when you can recognize your old story without giving it much thought, I want you to write a new story. Write the story of how you *wish* life was. How much fun you could have and how you could go all the places you want to go or do all the wonderful things you want to do. Then I want you to look at this new story every day. Spend time envisioning it in the morning, in the shower, or at night before you go to bed. Dream about it, live it over and over in your mind. If you catch yourself starting to tell your old story, quickly change your vision to your wonderful new story and see what happens for you.

It may seem silly now, but I'll ask you, what do you have to lose for trying? What will it cost you if you keep your old story? I don't know about you, but I've done this and my new story rocks!

Staying Strong in Your New Beliefs

I can honestly say from experience that if you do not do the work of being firm with your loved one and setting your new intentions for your life, they will quickly pull you back into their downward spiral. I saw this very thing happen recently in the story I shared about having my brother come and live with me last year. To recover from the downward spiral, I had to reach deep into my soul to find my next step forward and, as I reflected on where I want to go and what I want to do, I decided that writing this book and making it my destiny to help families who face addiction is the path I was chosen to be on. I felt this burning desire, a calling from source, to help people like you, who face family addiction, heal from the hurt.

Through doing this work and finding my inner peace once again, I now make it a point to go to bed every night, no matter how my day was, thanking the universe for everything that I have. Filling my thoughts with gratitude before sleep and looking forward to the next day's challenges. This is an amazing practice to set yourself up for a better night's sleep and waking in the morning in a better mood.

We who face these challenges in family addiction have to put in the work every day, despite our surroundings. Happiness is an *inside* job and it's the only way to manifest our desires to become destinies. I won't say it's easy, but I will say it's worth it. You are worth it!

By using the power of thought and visualization to change my life, I am happy despite it all ,and if I can do it, so can you.

Chapter 3. Healing Through Fear

"The only way to ease our fear and be truly happy is to acknowledge our fear and look deeply at its source. Instead of trying to escape from our fear, we can invite it up to our awareness and look at it clearly and deeply."

Thich Nhat Hạnh

Allowing Fear to Stop Us

I know that when it came to writing this next part, I almost didn't because of the very thing I want the most for you to bring to your awareness and get past – fear. Fear is what is at the bottom of all the excuses for not doing or being something in our lives. We can look at something we want to do and not do it and not even realize the deep reasons why. Writing this book, for example. So many times, I procrastinated out of fear. Fear is built into our minds and emotions to protect us. I want to go a bit more in depth about the two types of fear and the differences between them. These are good fear and bad fear.

Good fear keeps us from crossing the street without looking both ways. And good fear helps us to protect our children from things that may harm them. As parents, it is our job to teach our children about things they should fear so they can learn to protect themselves and not get injured.

As a side note, I find this ironic for those of us who have children in addiction because we have tried so hard to protect them from using drugs and alcohol, yet here we are on this hellish journey, wondering where we went wrong. When it's your child who is addicted, I think it feels natural to feel like you have failed as parents, but I ask you to STOP if you do feel this way, because it is not your fault, and those are limiting beliefs and fears. We do the best we can and raise our children as we know how to, right or wrong. It is up to them, as they become who they are, to ultimately figure it out, or, sadly, not. You can only control you and that is what the next step is. Really taking a look at where you are and what is truly stopping you from becoming who you want to be. Which is why we are going to talk about bad fear next.

The bad fear keeps you stuck and stops you from living the life you desire because of what you are experiencing with your loved one's addiction. Your mind is always creating stories of worry about your loved one and how awful this all is. You feel isolated and alone when they push against you for trying to help them. They are angry with you and lash out, so your story gets louder and louder in your mind and soon you can't think of anything else but replaying the scenes over and over. Worrying when they walk out the door, what they are going to do, if they will come home again. Fear is no place to live. It suppresses the joy you are meant to feel. When was the last time you felt truly happy?

I mentioned that I used to worry so much about my kids when they left the house without me. I'd visualize horrible things and have massive anxiety attacks until they returned. I couldn't function or focus on anything else until they walked through the door again. What a terrible way to live! This type of behavior is a huge red flag of codependency and living in fear.

When I didn't have control over their situation, it sent me into a panic. Once I learned that I have the power within me to change my thoughts, and with my newly awakened belief that there is a higher power watching over us, I found the strength to let go of what I cannot control. I was then able to release them with love and I would say this prayer to myself: *"Angels please watch over my children and keep them safe."* Then I would take a deep breath knowing they are safe and go about my day.

My kids are much older now but, even to this day, I say my prayer when I know they have to drive in bad weather or they are flying somewhere on vacation. I know it works, and they are safe, because they have each had very close calls with incidents over the years where they have said things like, "I don't know how..." or "I'm lucky that..." and I take a breath and say thank you to my angels for watching over them and keeping them safe.

Now that you have a prayer to keep your loved ones' safe why not make the decision to change from fear and hopelessness to joy and happiness right now, no matter what is going on?

When I asked you just now to decide to be happy no matter what your loved one was doing, what came up for you? Did you think, "Sure, why not?" or did you think ,"Are you kidding me? How do you expect me to be happy right now?"

As adults, we need to make decisions all the time. If we don't make a decision, we can't move forward. Sometimes we are afraid of the consequences if we do make a decision, and we feel it is easier to just not make one than it is to follow through when we do decide to do something because of our fears. Soon we find we are too late, or we are second guessing ourselves so much we that don't know how to get out of it. Some advice: lose the "what if's" and decide to be happy despite it all. What do you have to lose by deciding to be in a happy state instead of a fearful state? Or a worry state?

The Be Happy Anytime Exercise

Let's do an exercise right now to start shifting your mindset so you can decide to be happy any time you want. Please grab paper and a pen and write down all the things that do make you happy in your life. Then write down all the things you are afraid of or that you worry about a lot. Once you have a list of both I want you to look at the things that you fear and visualize those things happening, one at a time. Once you have a picture in your head of that fearful thing, I want you to replace it really quick with one of the things on your list that makes you happy and visualize that in your mind instead.

If you can get to a point where you can recognize your fearful or worry thoughts as they start to happen and quickly replace them with a thought that makes you happy, soon the fearful or worry thoughts will fade away and they won't come up for you as much. It takes awareness and practice, but it will work if you keep at it as a part of your "happy story" daily practice from the last chapter. Don't forget to journal about your experiences of how you are becoming aware of your worry or fearful thoughts and how it is getting easier to quickly change them and go into your "bubble life," a term I will explain later.

Doing the Work to Come Into Alignment With Your Inner Feelings

When we are doing things for others that don't feel good to us inside, we are out of alignment with source. These feelings cause us anxiety, fear, depression, and my favorite go-to feeling, anger. We are meant to feel happiness and love and not these other feelings that we live with everyday due to our loved one's addiction. We need to do the inner work to heal these feelings, and setting boundaries is the next step.

Breaking Through Fear and Setting Boundaries

"Love yourself enough to set boundaries. Your time and energy are precious. You get to choose how you use it. You teach people how to treat you by deciding what you will and won't accept." Anna Taylor

How many times has your loved one asked you for something and instead of saying "no," you said "yes"? Why? Was it out of guilt? Do you want to please them? Or are you afraid of their reaction if you tell them no?

Tough Love Instead of Fear

When we have a loved one in addiction, they ask a lot of us all the time and we need to decide whether or not we help them with those things we don't agree with, like giving them money when they call with a sob story. Or letting them back into our home again because they have nowhere else to go. They are really good at making us feel guilty, aren't they?!

You'll begin to define who you are and what your needs are when you decide to set boundaries with your loved one in addiction. It helps them to understand what you will tolerate and what you won't. You may be afraid to tell your loved one that you will not continue this journey with them because you want to see them sober and healthy again and you may feel like if they don't have you to help them anymore they won't ever get sober. It's so exhausting watching them hurt themselves and you. Maybe you've been through so much at this point that you feel like hating them for what they do to you. But if you stop "helping," or you force them to leave, what will happen to them? Do you feel anxious when you think about this? Does it often stop you from setting boundaries?

In the past, I always found it's easier to give in than to say no. I always wanted to say no, but instead I made the decision to help them every time even though it went against my inner-knowing and felt so wrong. I learned over time that tough love is hard, but it is also necessary to move forward with your own life. If we let emotions like fear stop us from giving them tough love, they will just ask for more and more and walk all over us. Tough love saves lives, yours and theirs.

Making the decision to say no despite the fear of what might happen to your loved one is a big step in taking back control of your life and moving forward. We can't let the emotions of fear, guilt, or regret stop us from saying, "no, enough is enough."

Even now, I have to use tough love with my brother. He asked me for money just recently. He said he didn't want to call me to ask but he doesn't know what else to do. It went something like this:

"I can't work because I broke my toe, I was going to go today but it's pouring rain and my boss is sick."

I said, "that's too bad, I'm sorry."

He said, "I hate to ask but if you could send me $50 it would really help, I'm hungry. I don't have any food, cigarettes or beer right now."

"Well I'm at work so there is nothing I can do right now. I can't go to Western Union and I'm not even sure I have any money I can send. You should go to the food pantry if you are that hungry to get something to eat."

His response was, "It's pouring and I have this hospital boot on, it's miles away and my foot would get wet."

I said, "Oh, sorry I don't know what to tell you."

My thoughts at this moment are: "Well if I Western Union $50, you would get your foot wet to go to the store and get the money!"

Later that day, I got a text from his girlfriend and it said, "I hope you can help Dan, he is really freaking out right now." So, I called him. I told him that I don't have the money to send and that they need to figure it out. He was sweet to me and says he will be okay ,even though he probably wasn't okay. He said he would just have to go to work tomorrow with his broken toe. It breaks my heart to say no, but I've decided that there is no amount of money I can throw at him that is going to make things okay. He has to do the work to make things better. I know inside that I have to be strong and stick to my decision. I can't let the fear of what might happen to him or the guilt that comes up because I said no stop me from detaching with love. If I were to break down and give him the $50 today, next week there would be another story, and another. I've been there and I am not going back.

It takes courage to detach with love because we do love them so much, but we also must reach a point where we have to be our own top priority. If we can't do that we will never move forward and we are losing this gift of life because we were too afraid to say no.

Doing the Work to Push Past Fear and Heal

In circumstances where you've said no and they either stormed out the door or they are out there somewhere and you don't know where, it's really hard to be happy and not worry about them. But with every storm is a chance to see the morning sunrise inside of you. Knowing that you are doing the best you can in your life, and that the behavior they are displaying is theirs to own, is the beginning of healing. Instead of feeling guilty or worried for them, concentrate on you. Who are you right now? What do you need to do to take care of yourself? Decide to push fear aside and, in that moment, find something about you and your life that makes you happy and sit with it for a few minutes. Go back to the exercise above. How do you feel when you think of something about you that is good or positive? That's the feeling you want to live in all of the time. There will be more storms with your loved one and there will be more beautiful sunrises if you decide to see them. You can tell yourself that you shouldn't feel happy because of the situation with your loved one and you can live your life in fear and worry, or you can decide to reach for something that brings you joy and become the person you are meant to be instead. What will you decide?

Self-Care

After we've set boundaries with our loved ones and they know what we will tolerate and what we won't, it's time to start changing our own thought patterns.

We need to be able to get enough sleep at night and not let these thoughts and feelings keep us awake instead. If we are not getting enough rest, it causes a ripple effect to our days. We don't tend to eat right, we don't want to exercise, or do what is best for us to get to that feeling of happiness and love for ourselves. And if you are like me, you take it out on everyone else around you.

I know that when something is bothering me and I'm stressed, I stop eating and go for nicotine and lots of coffee instead. My attitude sucks. I do "busy work" instead of being productive because I can't focus on myself and my needs.

When I'm recognizing that my thoughts and feelings are not in alignment with source, I quickly disrupt the negative patterns and change them to something that does feel good to me, and I am then able to shift my patterns. I become more productive. I exercise, and I eat right. I feel so much better when I can focus and not let what's going on out there affect me. I like to call this "bubble life." It sounds funny but when I'm in my "bubble," I am not affected by my surroundings. I am happy, I practice gratitude, and I recognize and appreciate the good that is coming to me.

When I'm out of my "bubble," I'm easily frustrated and the littlest thing sets me off. This is wasted energy. Getting upset and angry about something that has happened is useless. Whatever it was, it has already happened, and we can't go backwards, so why keep on about it? Instead, I've learned to ask, "what lesson can I learn from this?" When I sit in meditation and ask ,"what can I learn from this?", I wait for an answer, and if it doesn't come, then I pay attention and watch for signs in the coming days. I usually always get my answer when I watch for them and then I say thank you to the universe for the lesson.

Living your life in a state of gratitude ,"in your bubble," isn't always easy, but it is necessary in order to stay on your path and live your life the way it was meant to be, happy and peaceful.

Our thoughts can set us free or drag us down. My objective here is to help you become free to live your life and fulfill your destiny, to stop the hurt and begin to heal so you can be truly happy.

Our loved ones in addiction live in despair. Their days are dark, and depression prevails. We see this and have two choices: join them or rise above and be strong enough to be happy anyways. Are you living in despair and darkness along with your loved one? Or are you living in love and happiness?

Deciding to Rise Above

The decision to rise above is not always easy. This is where the real work begins. Self-love is so important. When is the last time you could look in the mirror and tell yourself "I love you"? Have you ever? I know that it is still hard for me, but once I started the healing process, the next step for me was to do just that. Healing begins when you have that moment of clarity about what your soul really wants for you versus where you are in your emotions right now. I think you will find that the mirror reflects back to you some pretty strong feelings you have about yourself at first. Take note of those feelings and you will know what you need to work on the most. Your inner self is hurting and until you know what is really broken, you can't fix it.

Daily Mirror Exercise and Journaling

Start today and do this every time you see your reflection in a mirror or catch a glimpse of yourself in a window. It may seem really silly at first, or it may seem really scary, but please do it anyways. I have taught this exercise in my group and some cried, some were relieved, and some were so grateful for having gone through this process. So take a self-care action right now and make sure you do this for you.

Stand in front of a mirror, look yourself right in the eyes, and say "<Your Name> I love you. I really love you."

Recognize the feelings that come up and just sit with them. Don't resist them. Embrace them. Then go and write them down in your journal. Do this every day for a week. Pay attention to how it feels on day one and then on day seven, go back through your journal and see how you have progressed with it during the week. Did it get easier each time? How did it make you feel? What can you start to work on in order to heal the emotions or pictures that come up inside of you?

Next, for week two stand in front of the mirror and say "<Your Name> I love you and I am so proud of you."

Remember to sit with the feelings and really pay attention to what comes up for you. Was it easy or hard to tell yourself how proud you are of yourself? Again, do this for a week, and then reflect on your progress on day 14 in your journal.

Keep going for week three and really get into this week. I want you to smile in the mirror while you say "I love you." Then get crazy with it and tell yourself how amazing you are and how you're going to crush your day. Don't forget to journal after. Maybe you are feeling more confident at work after doing this, maybe you catch the fact that you are smiling more around others. Just maybe, you feel lighter and happier.

Once we can truly accept ourselves as the amazing people we really are, we start to see the shift in how we do things and how we act around others. It builds confidence and character and, I will say this, that reflection you see every time you look in the mirror is amazing, you are amazing.

I found this on the Internet and wanted to share

Dear Self:

If you keep going backwards with the same people God has intentionally removed from your life, you will continue to stay stuck. There is no joy in being confused and unhappy. Get rid of old bad habits and leave them where they belong. What is meant for you will be yours, learn to let go. Dysfunction isn't love.

Sincerely,

Self

*found on <u>Google</u>

Chapter 4. Forgiveness and Serenity

Accepting and Serenity

"The Three C's: "When I accept that I didn't cause it, I can't control it, and I most certainly can't cure someone else I feel serenity." Quote from the Nar-Anon book, *SESH - Sharing, Experience, Strength, and Hope*

Accepting addiction for what it is and reaching a point of serenity is a blissful feeling. Becoming empowered is key in having the strength to continue to heal. It makes you more prepared for when your loved one calls you with a story about how awful things are for them or when they ask you again for money because they are hungry (but really, it's for a fix).

How do we stay serene through this? How do we continue to have the strength to say no? This work is part of what we are here to learn.

Here are some suggestions to help you when you don't feel like you can find the strength to be empowered:

- Take 10 minutes to do some deep breathing or meditation throughout your day.
- Write or journal your feelings.
- Take a walk or a drive in your car and just appreciate the view.
- Practice some positive affirmations.
- Create a vision board.

If you are not able to do any of these things due to time constraints or other excuses you may tell yourself, try to just practice recognizing the thoughts about how your loved one makes you feel, and change those thoughts to mirror how you want to feel. Daydream for a moment about what your life would be like once you start to heal and become empowered.

Here is an example of how I might use what we learned so far when a circumstance comes up that interrupts my "bubble life": *My loved one just called and said he's cold and hungry. What kind of a person am I to let this go on and not help? I should just let him/her come back."*

I changed this old thought practice to, "*I am strong and I pray for my loved one to be safe. I am doing what's right for me and I know they will find a way.*" The point is to get to a better-feeling place by replacing the old fear and guilt with strength and hope.

I personally took a step backwards when I allowed my brother to come and live with me. I fell prey to the heartache. I love my brother and even though he will never be sober, I wanted to try to help him anyways. I was able to help him get off heroin for the time he was with me, but he dragged me down in the process. I was completely out of my bubble. His drinking was costing me $100 a week. I felt guilty for buying his beer, but I did it anyway because he couldn't live without it, yet I hated how he acted once he had a buzz. I'd try to teach him what I've learned and show him how domesticated life could be, but it wasn't for him. All of my codependent behaviors came roaring back. Honestly, he really tried to listen and be different, but the years of hardcore drugs and drinking have made his brain a mess. It was like Groundhog Day over and over again. He has no short-term memory, but he can tell you stories from the past like they happened yesterday, some you could believe and some so far-fetched that only he could believe they were real. It was really hard to live with and I needed to take back control of my life and practice what I had learned.

I share this in hopes you will trust in yourself and no matter what your loved one does, love yourself enough to take back control of your life.

"THE MISCONCEPTION: If you are in a bad situation, you will do whatever you can do to escape it. THE TRUTH: If you feel like you aren't in control of your destiny, you will give up and accept whatever situation you are in." David McRaney

Self-Forgiveness and Forgiving Our Loved Ones

"Forgiving does not erase the bitter past. A healed memory is not a deleted memory. Instead, forgiving what we cannot forget creates a new way to remember. We change the memory of our past into a hope for our future." Lewis B. Smedes

It is easy for us to put the blame on ourselves for our loved one's addiction. Do you often say, "If I... then they might not have?" or "If I... then they may have?" Guilt is a huge part of addiction for both our loved ones and ourselves. We blame them, they blame us, and it goes around in a circle.

Breaking this cycle by doing the work of forgiveness is difficult but enlightening. When I read the book *Adult Children of Alcoholics* by Janet Weititz, I went through an exercise on forgiveness where I wrote a letter to some of the people who had hurt me in the past. I told them what they had done to hurt me, how it made me feel, and then I forgave them.

The intent of the exercise is not to give them the letter, but to free yourself by forgiving. You are not saying what they did was acceptable or right, because it most likely wasn't, but you are giving yourself permission to let it go and to become free from the pain it has caused you.

The people who hurt you probably never give a second thought to what you are feeling because of their actions. It is you who feels this pain and you who need to forgive. I know this won't be easy, but what I learned is that the people who hurt us were only doing what they knew to do, what they had learned as a child growing up, or what they had experienced themselves.

We are all offered teachings and experiences from our parents, teachers, or others, and we process what they have to offer and either accept it or choose to believe something different. I found that once I could forgive those who hurt me for what they did, it took such a load off of me. I felt so much lighter and free and I allowed myself to heal.

I used to go to bed at night and either spin these horrible thoughts or wake up out of a sound sleep because I jumped, dreaming about these things. Has this happened to you too?

I couldn't stop the memories from coming. I didn't want to relive the horror and the pain over and over again. Once I was able to go through this exercise and truly forgive myself and others who caused me pain, the thoughts stopped coming. I now can choose whether I want to drag them out and think about them, or not. Most of the time they just don't come up for me anymore.

I encourage you to try going through this exercise to see if it helps you too. Some people will actually give the person the letter, some will choose to keep it, and some will actually burn them in symbolism of becoming free. I kept mine in a notebook but, honestly, I don't even know where that notebook is anymore. The point is to become free, not to go back and relive it again and again.

Healing Your Inner Child

Did you know you have a little you inside?

No... not a baby but an inner child. I'd heard the term and blown it off for most of my life, but when I really started to embrace my inner power I found my "little Kelly" and I was able to meditate and just sit with her and see this little girl who told me how scared she was, how much she just wanted to be loved, and how she was hurting. I held this little girl and I told her she is loved. And not to be scared anymore. And that she is safe now. God, how that helped me heal! So powerful. Now when I see her, we laugh, swing, and just rock in peace and love.

What would your inner child have to say?

Meditation to Heal Your Inner Child

Try this exercise to begin forgiving yourself and your loved ones using meditation or visualization.

We all have a little version of ourselves inside and if we don't heal our little one, the process of forgiving ourselves won't be complete. There is a meditation, which I often use where you visualize yourself as a small child and you sit with your child and listen to them. They will tell you they are hurting. You can then visualize yourself as you are now, holding that small child, rocking them, and letting them know they are ok. You can tell them that they are loved and just forgive yourself for all the hurt this small child has endured. It feels so good to do this exercise.

You can also do this for your loved one in addiction. They didn't just wake up one day and become addicted. Chances are they are hurting too or have faced some trauma in their lives, which is causing them to want to numb the pain. By visualizing them as a small child, holding them, and telling them that they are loved and that you are here for them you will feel better. This exercise will help you to see through their eyes what is causing them to be who they are today so you can begin to forgive them for how they make you feel.

I keep a picture of myself as a small child on my dresser and when I'm feeling lost, I look at her and she makes me smile. She loves to swing and to laugh and sing. She reminds me of my journey and that I'm now living my destiny and it helps me to keep going.

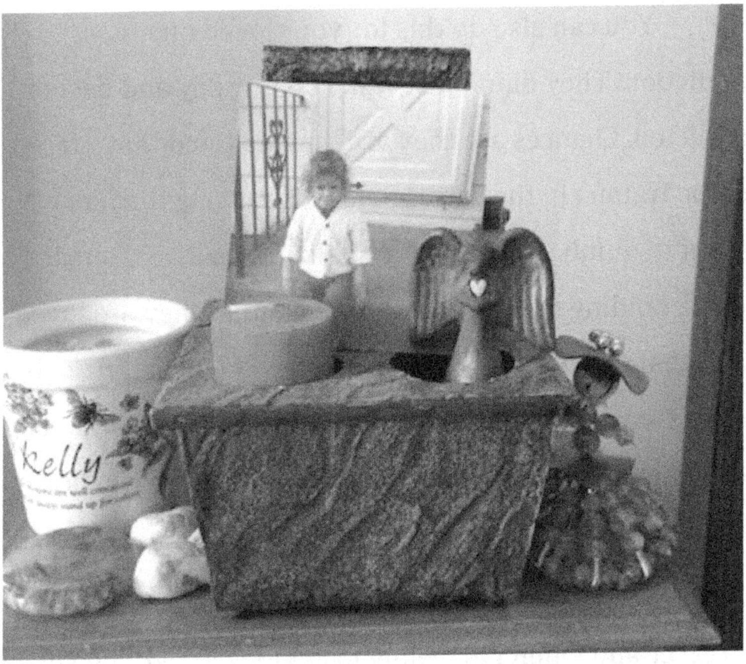
Kelly

Chapter 5. Trust in a Higher Power

"But I think that because they trusted themselves and respected themselves as individuals, because they knew beyond doubt that they were valuable and potentially moral units -- because of this they could give God their own courage and dignity and then receive it back. Such things have disappeared, perhaps because men do not trust themselves anymore, and when that happens there is nothing left except perhaps to find some strong sure man, even though he may be wrong, and to dangle from his coattails." John Steinbeck, *East of Eden*

In the beginning of this book, I explained my views on believing in a higher power and I have used various different terms throughout the chapters to describe this power, which, in a sense, are all the same thing. For those who think that the world and the unlimited universe just came to be, or that it is all purely scientific, that's fine, but frankly it's all just too perfect for there to not have been something, a higher power perhaps, through which it has all come to be.

I talked about how finding a higher power saved my life by allowing me to let go. I gave you examples of how I had to turn my power over to the angels and ask them to keep my children safe so I could stop the worry and negative thoughts I was creating when I didn't have control. This is faith. Faith is so powerful. You've heard that already, I'm sure, but have you actually lived it?

Have you prayed but found that your prayers were not answered, so you stopped believing? I have. Life was not pretty when I lost my faith. However, when my son got sick and I had nothing but faith to help me get through it, I knew it was the answer to all things. The law of attraction is real and will give you whatever you desire as long as you have the absolute faith that what you seek is already yours. This is probably the most difficult thing anyone has ever been asked to do, yet there are those like Buddha, Mother Teresa, Gandhi, and Jesus who have shown us that faith can move mountains if we don't let our free will to think or act in any other way get in the way of it.

If you are familiar with the 12 steps of AA, you'll know that they use the word "God," but they also speak of a spiritual awakening. There are many terms used today for "God," so I want you to use whatever you are comfortable with. We may agree to disagree about our beliefs about God, but I ask you to stay with me again where it's hard and hear me out. What I want you to be open to is this: your soul inside of you is God. We are spiritual beings in a human body having an experience. So, God inside of all of us is our soul.

I've alluded to how I change my thoughts and when I am not in my "bubble" I am disconnected from this higher power. We think over 60,000 thoughts a day. We can choose to believe these thoughts and take them all as literal, or we can make up our minds to change them. But what about when you are conflicted in your mind? Do you ever have a time when you are arguing with yourself? Who is that inside that you are arguing with?

Soul Self vs Ego Self

We talked a lot about fear and how we get caught up in worry thoughts and negativity in our own minds. We have good fear and bad fears built into us. But do you know where these fears come from? This is our Ego mind. It has one job – to keep us safe. The flight or fight response is real. When we live in our Ego mind, we want security and safety. These things are nice but if that's all you have then while the rest of the world is out there crushing it, you find yourself left behind in a corner because you are choosing to let your Ego keep you safe.

The Ego wants to always be right.

Have you had conversations or arguments with your loved ones where you believe you are right and nothing that they say matters because you know you are right? This too comes from Ego. Ego holds us back in believing something else to be true because Ego always has to be right. Humility and being a kinder being comes when you can listen to others and accept that what they are saying reflects their beliefs about being right, and then letting it go. Take this topic for example. You may have a strong belief that there is not a higher power and have closed your mind to the idea. This comes from your Ego mind. So, if this is you please keep reading

Soul Self and Intuition

"Authentic inspiration endows individuals with mental or spiritual energy which they are then able to transform into positive action. It can make all the difference between a man, woman, or child allowing despair to permanently paralyze any dreams they may have for their lives, or, exercising sufficient strength of will to make those dreams a reality." Aberjhani, *Journey through the Power of the Rainbow: Quotations from a Life Made Out of Poetry*

We all have what's called intuition. Maybe you have experienced a time where something just didn't feel right inside and you didn't go somewhere or do something and later found out that there was a bad accident and you realized if you had been there, that it could have been you. For me, it was that voice telling me to wear my seatbelt because I was going to get in an accident.

But where do these feelings or thoughts come from? We all know that the earth and the entire universe are made up of energy and everything is vibrating. We interpret these vibrations as reality in our minds. That is so powerful. But because we are here on this energetic vibrational planet, doesn't that too mean that we are energy that is vibrating in step with the rest of the universe? That we are somehow connected to this higher vibration and energy? Our bodies are a vehicle to hold these things together, to have experiences and learn from the contrast we call "problems" in our lives. Our inner guidance is this very energy, and it wants only love and grace for us. Our souls hold the key to our destiny, and it is up to us to quiet our Ego mind and choose to hear it and follow it.

How do we listen to something we don't realize is there when we are caught up in the day-to-day things we call life? One way is meditation. Practicing sitting quiet and getting your thoughts to slow or even stop for a time and just listening. You will hear what you need to hear if you trust in what shows up for you in this state.

Often people will chalk things like this up to coincidence. I wrote off that voice telling me to wear my seatbelt, justifying it as guilt. But, as I became aware of the fact that intuition is real and there are signs out there to watch for when something comes up for me, I began to pay attention.

Let me give you another example. One morning in my old apartment I was washing my hands in the kitchen sink. The water seemed extra hot for some reason. I went about my routine of getting ready and was putting on my coat when I heard, "You need to go down to the cellar and check the water heater" in my mind. I could have shrugged it off and left, but remembering that I need to trust that voice and have faith, I went downstairs, knowing that traffic was building up the longer I wasn't on the road. When I turned the corner at the bottom of the stairs, I found that the basement was flooded. The water heater had broken. It was a gas water heater and, if I had blown that voice off, the outcome probably would not have been the same. Because I took the action and listened to that voice, I was able to call my landlord and have someone come service it that morning.

I've also learned that when we pray, just because we don't see immediate answers doesn't mean we shouldn't stop looking for clues or signs that our prayers were heard. Little things throughout our day that occur have meaning if we know what to look for. Recurring number patterns all have messages for us. We often see 444, 555, 11:11 on the clock, license plates, or elsewhere. If you know that when you see those, they are signs, you can look up your answers right on Google. Try it. Next time you see a recurring number Google whatever the numbers were like this: "555 meaning." See if the message there has any relevance to what you are going through in your life at that time. I love to do this because it helps me to know when I'm on the right path or when I should be looking out for something that may be coming in my life that I might not be expecting.

When we ask for something, whether out loud or to ourselves, the universe hears this and delivers. You may be thinking, I've asked for several things and haven't gotten them. I'll challenge that with, or have you, but your thoughts are not aligning with what you're asking for? What I mean by this is, say you pray to win a million dollars and you go and buy a lottery ticket. The numbers come out, but you didn't win. What's your next thought? Is it, "see I knew I wouldn't win, I never win anything," or is it more like "ok, so I didn't win this time, but I know because I've asked to win, if I keep trying and believe it to be true, I'll win one day." Do you see the difference? This is not probably the most realistic example, but I hope I got the point across about how we ask for things and to hold faith in our hearts that what we ask for will be answered.

    If we ask and then cancel out what we ask for because we don't believe we can have it, it can't come. But if you affirm and hold onto the vision of what it would feel like when it happens and never waiver, it will happen. From my experience, it may not look exactly like what you asked for, but it could be even better. I'm not making claims that you will win the lottery. This is just one example to get you thinking about what you are asking for, and how to create a means for it to happen. By believing in what you are asking for and holding onto that belief without allowing a negative thought to cancel it out, it has to come.

The opposite can be true as well. When we see our loved ones acting in wrong behavior by using drugs or alcohol and we only focus on what they are not doing right, we attract more of that into our lives as well. Do your best to find a vision of your loved one in recovery and happy, put your focus there instead of on what happened in the past or where they are right now in their journey.

My Journey with the Law of Attraction and Absolute Faith

My real-life example of this saved my son's life. This story is lacking in many details and I've spoken with my son about sharing my story. He doesn't want his past out there but has given me a chance to share some of it in hopes we can help others. He doesn't even know to this day the horror I experienced mentally to help him through what I'm about to share with you.

A few years ago, my son developed drug-induced schizophrenia and psychosis. His behavior was abnormal, and I had no idea what mental health issues really looked like. He was your typical troubled teen, drinking, smoking pot, and experimenting with other narcotics (sorry to stereotype). What I didn't know, I didn't know, but the signs were all there. Needless to say, we went on a wild ride that particular summer and I found myself very alone. No matter where I reached out, no one would help me to help him. No one believed me when I said he was sick. He could speak coherently but his actions were not his typical actions at all. Because he was an adult, medically there was nothing I could do. He didn't know he was sick, so when I tried to legally help him, he was able to talk his way out of it every time, and even tell the authorities I was crazy. And they believed him!

On this journey, he was out there alone for several weeks, not realizing he was sick. I was trying to work and maintain my duties at home while struggling to get him help, which was so difficult because I didn't even know where he was. He left his apartment with no wallet, no phone, and no money. It was a mother's worst nightmare to know that no matter where you turn, no one will help you. I prayed every day and every night while this was going on. I had reported him missing and even posted it on Facebook. I was desperate to help him but the only thing I had was prayer and the knowledge I learned from a book titled T*he Game of Life and How to Play It* by Florence Scovel Shinn. The Game of Life is just that, a game. You create it through your thoughts, actions, and beliefs. So I started to pray at every turn on this journey, saying to myself over and over again, "I see my son getting the help he needs in a perfect way." I'd repeat this over and over again and if a negative thought came, I would stop it and just keep repeating this line day and night, never wavering in my belief that he would get the help he needed.

    One day after many weeks of trying to get my son help, I finally got the call. Usually we don't want these calls about our kids, but this one was a good one! He was captured by the right officials for the last time. These officials were trained in mental illness and understood that he was sick. For his actions in today's world, he is lucky that they were trained in mental illness or he could have been shot. He didn't do anything really horrible, just something that proved he was not thinking coherently.

The next step was to convince the DA, a judge, and the court counselors that he was experiencing mental illness and that what he did was due to this, that he needed help.

When I reached the courthouse, where the officials had brought him, it was after 2pm and court was over for the day. I met the DA first and explained that my son was sick, which he in turn told the judge. When they brought my son before the judge, I could see every bone in his spine from the neck down. He had been aimlessly wandering the streets in an adjacent state from where we lived for days. When the judge asked him his name, he stated that he was John Smith from Smithfield. This proved to the judge that he wasn't coherent, however, since it was so late in the day the counselors had gone off site and it would be two days before we could get another court date to have them evaluate him. The judge had no choice but to send him to prison for holding and I had to go home and wait. At least he was finally safe.

All the way home and for the next two days, every waking minute I repeated over and over again, "I see the judge helping my son in a perfect way!"

I returned to the courthouse two days later and brought a notebook with me, which I used to document the whole journey, to plead my case and get my son help. On that day he was finally sent to a hospital where he stayed for three weeks. I was eternally grateful to the officials and the court for believing in me and for helping my son.

Today he is still battling with alcohol, but the schizophrenia and psychosis have not returned. He knows he has an issue and I pray every day that he will win his battle. I am powerless over his addiction, but I know in my heart that he will overcome this when he is ready. It is my belief that if I didn't have this knowledge, things could have turned out very differently.

This may still sound like a stretch to you, but one day if you meet me and you hear the whole crazy story, you'll agree that because I kept my faith and believed in the outcome I wanted, that this "game" really does work!

I've also used visualization and affirmations for my own personal things as well, such as manifesting my first new home even with horrible credit and getting two promotions at work in one year. Unfortunately, I can't make the traffic move, but I can tell you that if you still don't believe there is more to us than just our bodies living on this planet, try to put some of what I teach here into practice for yourself.

This one may also seem like a stretch, but I think it's really cool and worth mentioning here. Spirit animals carry a message for us as well. Pay attention to animals you may see in your day or in an image somewhere. Spirit animals all have meaning, and we are all connected in this energy so if you see a hawk, for example, Google "Hawk Spirit Meaning" and see what comes up for you. Common everyday animals such as squirrels and chipmunks have messages too, but since we see them all the time it's less likely to be a communication. However, if you catch a rare glimpse of an eagle or hawk, or something you wouldn't normally see every day, there is probably a message there for you.

My strangest example of this was again at that same apartment while my son was sick. On the outside of the screen in the kitchen were about 20 house flies. I looked out the window for some reason, and saw them all just walking around on the screen. I had never experienced this before, so I googled "fly spirit animal." Here is the message of the fly: "Much like the butterfly, the fly symbolizes letting you know that quick and abrupt changes in your thoughts, emotions, and endeavors are afoot. Moreover, these rapid changes in all aspects of your life are happening now. Therefore, you should be prepared to move quickly even in unfavorable and uncomfortable conditions. Similar to the rabbit, fly meaning can also signify that an exponentially growing source of abundance is available for you right now. Thus you must use your keen eyesight to see the way. In other words, never give up." Now depending on what I was going through at that time, this may have been a message I didn't want to miss, and I sure didn't want to miss it. Never give up in a time of such uncertainty was the message I was meant to hear. And the strangest part was that once I read the message, they all disappeared.

We have all heard of "pennies from heaven" and feathers we find are our deceased loved ones letting us know they are here. There are so many signs and answers we seek coming from the universe, we just need to have faith and be awake enough to see them.

It's hard to explain and may sound silly to you but I ask you to pay attention throughout your days. Especially if you have been asking for something and want change in your life. These are guides from the universe to help you find the answers you seek.

My Thoughts on the Bible

I like to think of the Bible as a playbook for life. All the answers we ever seek are right in there. To be honest, I was brought up Catholic and going to Church every Sunday to listen to them read the same verses from Passover to Christmas didn't do much for me. I didn't read the Bible because the way the words are written didn't make sense to me. It wasn't until I was awakened through my spiritual beliefs that I found that everything

I need to live a happy, well-balanced life in harmony is right there.

The Ten Commandments taught to me as a kid were strict rules, and my family said that if I didn't practice them, I was bad. As a young adult I left the Catholic practices and lost God. As I started to do the healing work as an adult and sought out my own spiritual journey, I learned how to change my thoughts and to believe in a higher power deep inside of me. I realized that God was in fact what makes up my soul and that is where my answers and intuition come from. Now when I look at the Bible, I can see that the Ten Commandments were meant as perfect advice to living a more fulfilled life. Let's face it, if you do something wrong and expect life to be good for you, then you are fooling yourself. These ten steps were put there as a guide for us to find all the peace and harmony, success and fulfillment in our lives, if we choose to follow them. That's the caveat, right? We also have free will to do, be, or think whatever we want, thus the need for a life playbook such as the Bible. It is a tool and a guide and when the lessons are broken down into terms we can understand in today's world, I've found all the answers ever sought by man are right there in those pages. Amazing.

Right after I wrote this words above, I got a notification on my phone. It was a message from my Bible phone app, the verse of the day was Psalm 139:13-16 KJV:

> For thou has possessed my reins: thou hast covered me in my mother's womb. [14] I will praise thee; for I am fearfully and wonderfully made: marvellous are thy works; and that my soul knoweth right well. [15] My substance was not hid from thee, when I was made in secret, and curiously wrought in the lowest parts of the earth [16] Thine eyes did see my substance, yet being unperfect; and in thy book all my members were written, which in continuance were fashioned, when as yet there was none of them.

Seriously, I couldn't make that up if I tried. Do you see how that message relates to what I was explaining to you above?

We ask and it is given; knowing what signs to look for when we ask in prayer and watching for them will give us the clues and answers we seek. Open your eyes and your heart in faith, and life will give you everything you ask for.

You are a spiritual being learning lessons in human form. Grow from your past lessons because we are never done learning and growing unless we choose to be. If you're still here with me, I believe you want to heal and grow. If you, because you are learning, go through a rough lesson, go within again to forgive yourself and sit with your higher power. Do the visual work to see what this lesson has to teach you, and then visualize the guilt, anger, or whatever the feeling is for you, and set it free.

When you are feeling anxious or worried, try to visualize any form of higher power that works for you. Know that this higher power is there to protect your loved ones and let go of the thoughts that are causing you to worry and live in fear. Have faith and let go. You are more than welcome to use my little prayer about the angels for yourself and your family as well if it helps. I'm not suggesting that you have to believe in angels, but I'll tell you that, for me, this belief gets me through every day.

I have skimmed just the surface of my beliefs and how they show up in my life every day. I hope this gives you some insight and that you will consider them in your day-to-day life when something triggers you. Keep faith in your soul strong and you will find everything you seek.

Chapter 6. Get a Support System!

"What is home? My favorite definition is "a safe place," a place where one is free from attack, a place where one experiences secure relationships and affirmation. It's a place where people share and understand each other. Its relationships are nurturing. The people in it do not need to be perfect; instead, they need to be honest, loving, supportive, recognizing a common humanity that makes all of us vulnerable." Gladys Hunt, *Honey for a Child's Heart: The Imaginative Use of Books in Family Life*

In the darkness we feel alone, isolated, and see no way out. When we are living with a loved one in addiction it can feel like this. Having the support of a professional, a coach, or understanding family and close friends can pull you out of this darkness and into the light.

We want so badly for our loved ones to seek help to recover and, when in recovery, to stay recovered. But what about you? What are you doing for support? Do you have a counselor or a life coach you can reach out to when you need someone?

I see so many stories of families reaching out in a support group I belong to on Facebook. It breaks my heart to see the heartache each of them is going through. It's a great place to start to get support, but if you truly want to heal and live your life as you design it, instead of being controlled by your loved one's addiction, you may want to consider some more professional help as well.

There are support groups for addicts but there are also support groups for the families as well. But maybe you are not comfortable with going to a meeting because you are afraid to walk through the door. Don't let fear hold you back. You may just find the help you need waiting on the other side. It's not for everyone, but everyone should try it at least once.

If you feel that support groups just aren't for you, counseling may be a good fit for you. Your physician may be able to give you a referral to a family counselor in your area. I know I went to counseling as a teen and it really helped me become stronger.

You could also consider a life coach. This is someone who you can talk to, receive advice from, and trust in confidence to be there for you in a less formal environment than a counseling session. I've done lots of one-on-one coaching and found it to be very enlightening, it even inspired me to become a life coach myself. I have recently formed a group coaching session called The Healing From Codependency MasterMind, where, you guessed it, a meeting of the minds happens. People just like you and I work on things together and it feels more like talking with your family as you discover your deepest fears and how to move forward with your life by overcoming the obstacles that are holding you back. This is my favorite way to get and give support. It's fun and informative. We work on the things that are suggested by the members of the group and everyone learns from everyone else's experiences.

One of my goals is to build a massive community of families who have healed their lives and overcome the heartache of addiction. Where everyone is thriving and shining their light for the world to see. I hope you will be there with us! We need you!

Personally, I have a couple of resources I have found very helpful in my own recovery. This first one was very useful to me because when I started researching codependency for this book, I realized how many traits I still have and need to work on myself!

CoDA - Codependents Anonymous (http://coda.org/): CoDA uses 12 traditions and offers meetings in person or online.

I also have to give credit to my dear friend, who walks family addiction with me, for introducing me to Learn 2 Cope, which is a group for families who face opioid addiction and the effects it has on us. These people have become family and helped me through my crisis with my son, as well as also being there to support me when my brother was living with me. You can find more information about L2C at learn2cope.org. They offer a 24-hour message board for support and local meetings.

I hope I have given you some helpful resources for finding healing in your journey through living life with a loved one in addiction and a good support system to assist you in the healing process. Please see the back of the book for more resources. I am looking forward to serving you in the future as a fellow codependent and as a life coach, if you so choose to join me!

About The Author

Kelly Craig is a devoted mother, sister, and friend. She takes pride in her growth in overcoming codependency. Kelly is a #1 best-selling co-author of *Still Beautiful: How to Discover Your Value, Self-Worth & the Self-Love Formula* by Kelly Falerdeau. Kelly and other co-Authors share how they have overcome tragic obstacles to realize their beauty within.

Through Kelly's journey of family addiction, she has learned to use spiritual practices to heal her life. She has seen the power of inner healing through self-love. Kelly is now dedicated to helping families who are on this hellish journey with their loved one in addiction. She invites you to find your inner joy once again. Kelly's Survival Guide and practices will allow you to heal your despair and hopelessness just as she has.

Kelly lives in Shrewsbury, Ma. as an empty nester with her rescue animals, Snapple, Manny, Chachi (the cats), and Bohdi the rescue pup.

Heal Your Life – Stay in Touch with Kelly!

YouTube: https://www.youtube.com/c/KellyCraig72
Facebook: https://www.facebook.com/kellycraigbrands
Twitter: https://twitter.com/coachkelly72
Pinterest: https://www.pinterest.com/kellycraigbrands/
Instagram: https://www.instagram.com/kellycraigbrands/
LinkedIn: https://www.linkedin.com/in/kellycraig72/

Amazon Author Page:

https://www.amazon.com/author/kellycraig

OTHER BOOKS BY KELLY CRAIG

Co-author #1 Best Seller - Still Beautiful: How to Discover Your Value, Self-Worth & the Self-Worth Formula
https://amzn.to/2RyssuY

Hire Kelly To Speak at Your Event!

Book Kelly Craig as your Keynote Speaker and You're Guaranteed to Make Your Event Highly Educational and Unforgettable!

For over two decades, Kelly Craig has been educating, and helping families find hope, faith, and courage in living with addiction.

Her origin story includes overcoming obstacles in living with family addiction with her Mom, Dad, Brother, and even her own son. She touches on how she was able to find hope, faith, and courage to change her life from one of negativity, despair, anxiety and depression to now living a positive, productive, happy, successful life.

Her unique style inspires, empowers and captures the audience's hearts, while giving them the tools and

strategies they need and want to heal and flourish while coping with a loved one in addiction.
For more info, visit http://kellycraigbrands.com/contact/

One Last Thing...

If you enjoyed this book or found it useful, I'd be very grateful if you'd post a short review on Amazon. Your support really does make a difference and I read all the reviews personally so I can get your feedback and make this book even better.

If you'd like to leave a review, then all you need to do is click the review link on this book's page on Amazon here:

https://www.amazon.com/gp/product/B0862FM6LV/ref=dbs_a_def_rwt_hsch_vapi_tkin_p1_i0#customerReviews

Thanks again for your support!

Thank You

To my readers,

I'm so glad you found this book and I hope it helps you on your journey to finding all the happiness and joy you seek in your life. As a special gift from me to you here is:

Made in the USA
Middletown, DE
26 July 2024